WRITING FAMILY HISTORY:
REFLECTIONS FIVE YEARS ON

CLARE BLATCHFORD · DIANA DEVLIN · SUSIE GUTCH
MARGARET MCALPINE · TRACEY MESSENGER · BARBARA SELBY
VANITA SHARMA · PATRIZIA SORGIOVANNI · NICOLA STEVENS
CLARE TRAVERS · KRISTINA TZANEFF

Writing Family History:
Reflections five years on

Cover design & book layout: Martin Stanley
www.martinstanleydesign.com

Contents

INTRODUCTION

In January 2011, a group of women met on a six-month 'Writing Family History' course run by the Faber Academy at the historic headquarters of the publisher in Bloomsbury, London. We came from varied backgrounds, each with a story we wanted to tell. Our tutor, Andrea Stuart, was about to publish her own family memoir and we hoped to learn much from her experience.

Over the six months, we learnt about research sources, thought about the many different ways of structuring our stories and tried out short pieces of writing on the group. It was wonderful to find out about each other's projects and to share an enthusiasm for family history with like-minded individuals.

In the summer of 2012, we launched an anthology of extracts from our writing projects at the Faber Academy and were thrilled that friends, family members and a number of agents attended. It felt like something of a milestone – a wider public knew what we were up to. For some of us, it felt like the start of something big – as Patrizia Sorgiovanni reflects in her piece in this anthology, we would soon be published writers, earning our living from our sparkling, award-winning narrative non-fiction!

While such lofty ambitions may not yet have been realized, five years on many of us are still labouring away at our projects, some nearer completion than others. The nature of some projects has changed entirely, as their authors describe in their contributions to this anthology. Group members have taken subsequent courses; new discoveries have led to changes of direction.

Yet what is amazing is that many of the participants in that original course five years ago have continued to meet together. What is more, in that time, we have launched a blog to showcase our research and writing, and have a Facebook page. Since we started collecting statistics in March 2013, the blog has been visited 13,585 times by 10,348 people. Pages have been viewed 24,170 times. Forty-four per cent of our readers are from the UK followed by seventeen per cent from the USA, but people from 139 countries have visited.

The discipline of writing regular blog posts has helped a number of us to keep going and even enabled us to connect with family members and others with useful information.

This anthology includes our reflections on our experiences of working on our projects over the last five years: what we've learned, and where we hope to go to from here on in.

We would like to thank Martin Stanley for his time and expertise in making the ebook available.

We continue to enjoy meeting together, learning from one another and critiquing each other's work. Long may it continue - although it would be good to get those projects finished at some point!

Tracey Messenger
Editor
On behalf of the Writing Family History group

Website: www.writingfamilyhistory.com
Facebook: fb.me/WritingFamilyHistory
Twitter: @writingfamily

CLARE BLATCHFORD

Five years, and what has been achieved? I speak only for myself, but where, oh where, is the story of my family's history? Not with the printers, that much is certain. But nonetheless there has been some travelling, and something learned.

When I considered joining the Writing Family History group I was possessed only by the vague idea that I wanted to put down something of the past, but I wasn't quite sure at first that my intentions were aligned with what the course promised. At least now I'm certain of what I'm doing and what it's all about, even if no script has been submitted to an agent or even to an e-publisher.

A written family history traditionally appears to be one of two things. The first is for publication, and for public consumption. For this it must be exciting; it must be sufficiently readable to grab the attention of a stranger; it must enable the reader to feel the woes that befell your ancestors through their journey from rags from riches, or perhaps their downfall from the heights.

Which of us has the skill to write this story? Many have done it, but I suspect that more have failed. Many people think that they have a story to write – a novel perhaps, and some around their forbears. It's easy enough to find one's own ancestors to be interesting, but to make them so to other people takes a rare talent. It's not enough to be good with words; one must also have the creative skills that can turn fact into a story worth reading. The road to success is often littered with the corpses of rejected scripts.

What of the second kind of family history? You may delve into your history for the family interest, capturing the past for future generations, and focusing your research on recorded fact. The purpose of this is to be more of a record than a story in its own right. It could be seen as a sort of written family tree, which is a good reference point when our children ask 'Where do I come from?' or 'Where do I fit in to the scheme of things?' Many young people turn their backs on their past, and usually only half listen when their elders talk about their grandparents or family happenings of the past. But they may have a change of heart when they are older, and then it might be too late. Many of us regret not having asked about the lives of our elders when they were still with us.

All this have I been thinking over the last five years. I am confident now that I write for the record, but as such I write only of my own experiences and of those around me. Eventually I've accepted that I write only about my own past - our past. I suppose I'm writing a memoir but is it family history? Yes, it is, I have decided, for I too am 'family', but there's more to it than that.

I, my children and several generations of ancestors, come from a very different life from the one we now enjoy in Britain. Although this country has changed in the time that we have lived here, this is as nothing compared to the difference we found when we moved from South Africa to Britain in the late 1970s. We had left behind a world still redolent of colonial living with its servants and its conceptions about the 'home' country, and were largely unaware of the subtle variations that are imposed by distance – of both geography and time. Here we met a difference in values and attitudes as much as of lifestyle.

My ancestors moved from England to the British colony of Natal at the height of the Empire. Several were missionaries, while others were what we might call 'economic migrants'. My husband however, was English of origin and this allowed us to come back to these shores when the scales fell from our eyes and the realities of the Apartheid regime became explicit. Life in KwaZulu/Natal (as it is now called) was very sweet on the surface, but there was an underlying sourness inseparable from the delights of climate, scenery and privilege. Deciding to leave was easy, but actually doing it less so. Leaving a familiar world is often painful, and for us, much was lost in the move. There was not only the loss of family – extended as well as immediate – but also of a wider sense of belonging. Most of all, moving countries permanently puts personal identity at risk. Anyone who has done this is likely to know what we experienced. Over time a lost way of life, even one's former self, become a memory.

It is interesting that when our family get together we seldom if ever, talk about former times, or 'the (supposedly) good old days'; and there's a tacit recognition that our loss is too painful to put at risk by 'opening up'. We avoid the past, concentrating on life as it now is, how we are doing and what the future might bring. But we have not forgotten that

Apartheid was an obscenity, and are sensitive to the risks of racial tyranny. We did the right thing, however much was lost.

Our new country required us to adapt to its culture, and in so doing we inevitably lost something of ourselves, for which we mourn. A recollection of that life – slipping from our grasp with the passing years – becomes important, and it is therefore the history of our immediate family, rather than the distant historical one, that has become compelling.

But we are not alone; statistics show that one in three Londoners was not born in the United Kingdom; we are a nation infused with newcomers. Migration has already become the modus vivendi of our present world, and many will have had the same experiences as we have had, of leaving a world behind – a world where people knew your origins and you knew where you belonged. True belonging means not having ever to ask the question; your place is self-evident and it is only when you find yourself alone that the question arises.

I therefore beseech others to recall the lives they have left behind before it is lost to their memories, and therefore to their children. To re-create that life in your writing may itself be a therapy, but is also important for your children and your children's children. So when, as they must, they become curious about their origins and or their ancestry, their curiosity will not be frustrated.

If all else fails, and your progeny never turn their heads round to ask questions about their background, (and I venture that they should be interested, since it is in fact, their own backdrop), your record could still be of interest to some future archivist, looking for instance, into twentieth-century post-colonial life in a far corner of the world. As the gap widens between the 'then' and the 'now' it becomes ever more important to recall that far world. And so I write on.

Clare Blatchford *is a fourth-generation South African who has lived in Britain for the last 40 years. She largely avoided her earlier educational opportunities, until at the age of 36, she enrolled at Natal University to study Sociology and Philosophy, later teaching Sociology as a Masters graduate. The Sociology department attracted the unwanted attention of BOSS – the South Africa regime's secret service. Claire became a radical opponent of Apartheid and the regime, until she and her family emigrated in 1977. Clare's project is to record the life of her South African family and their servants as the era of white privilege was ending.*

DIANA DEVLIN

The first day of my research into my grandfather's Casson family was exciting. I went to pick up six eighteenth- and nineteenth-century portraits from a man in Clevedon, Somerset, whom I had never met before. I had acquired them by the skin of my teeth. My name is not 'Casson'; the owner had contacted a cousin who does bear the name, to see if any member of the family was interested in buying them. Only at the last minute, when he was about to put them into an auction, did she forward his final message, convinced that she had told me about them months before. Four of them now hang on the stairs of a Yorkshire house, the only family home big enough to accommodate them. The other two, depicting, it has to be said, an incredibly wooden-looking couple, have been consigned to a cupboard.

Until then, those portraits were 'unknown unknowns'. More often I have been investigating 'known unknowns'. My search has brought me some fascinating encounters as I set about looking for places that my ancestors knew. On a walk in North Wales, where my branch of the Cassons lived for 150 years, I came across a Welsh Tudor house that was being excavated. The archaeologist was there, working on it. He showed my companion and me around the site, and then asked, in a friendly sort of way, 'What brings you to this part of the world?' We explained we were from the family that owned the first slate quarry in Ffestiniog, and I said that I was researching them. 'But', I confessed, 'I don't even know where they lived.' 'I know *exactly* where they lived,' he said, with his emphatic Welsh intonation. The next day, we drove up to Llan Ffestiniog, and met him outside St Michael's Church. There, in pouring rain, he showed us several Casson graves, including those of Catherine Casson, who had married one of our ancestors, and of her two small children. All of them, I learnt for the first time, had died only a year or so after the wedding, leaving the poor husband a widower for the rest of his life. Our guide took us to the piece of land where once had stood *Ty Uchaf*, the inn that the Cassons ran before the slate quarry began to make money. And he pointed us in the direction of *Blaen-y-ddôl,* which they bought when they became prosperous, at first a farmhouse, later a substantial mansion. Since then, I've returned several times, taking the drive from the road, visualising how it was festooned with arches and banners for family weddings, and how, on several occasions, quarriers and villagers lined the road to watch respectfully as a coffin of one of the Cassons was carried to the churchyard.

On the trail of a family legend, I once scrambled my way up to a disused slate quarry in the Lake District. My grandfather had told me how, when Bonnie Prince Charlie was coming south in his attempt to gain the British throne and had come within a few miles, his great-great-grandfather had hidden his long-case clock up there to keep it safe from looters, retrieving it after the Young Pretender's defeat. On that occasion, my companion was a local resident who guided me up the fell. While I rested, out of breath, on a rock, he went further up, to the caverns carved out of the slate, where a clock might well have been concealed. Later, in the pub, he regaled the assembled company with our exploit. 'I heard the clock ticking,' he insisted, and I dare say they are still telling the tale.

I have sat on the verandah at Plas Penrhyn, on a hillside near Portmeirion, in Gwynedd, looking out across a plain towards Porthmadog. My great-grandfather was married from that house. Before that, Elizabeth Gaskell used to visit one of her relatives there. Later, it was the home of Bertrand Russell. Taking tea with the present owner, I marvelled how, as soon as I heard her name, I realized I had known and admired her late mother-in-law, back in England. These serendipitous discoveries are amongst the incidental pleasures of research.

In Denbigh, the owners of the house where my grandfather spent his childhood, his father being manager of a local bank, showed me a small metal shoe they had found in the garden. I had only just read that his mother used to carry the smaller children in a donkey-cart round the town; perhaps the shoe had belonged to the donkey.

Last November, on my way back to Richmond from Wales, where I had been doing further research, I made a detour to Keele University to read an MA Thesis that might provide further information about a mining engineer who had married into the Casson family. (Whereas doctoral dissertations can often be digitalised and downloaded, an MA thesis is usually only available as a hard copy.) Imagine my frustration when, after hanging around in the Library for an hour, a member of staff confessed that, having put it aside for me the day before, he now could not find it! Swallowing my annoyance, I checked my watch and realized that I now had time, before continuing my journey home, to drive a few miles north to Sandbach. I had never managed to locate the family house outside the town where some of those portraits had first hung. Surely, now that I had a satnav, I could find it. Alas no, I found the farm next door to it, but was still at a loss to see where the house was. Two men were chatting in a barn. 'Can you tell me where Betchton House is?' I asked. My luck was in. Not only was one of them the owner, but when I explained that I was having difficulty finding the date when it had ceased to be owned by the Cassons, the answer was immediately forthcoming. 'The house was sold to my father in 1919,' he explained, as he showed me into the elegant eighteenth-century hall. That date made perfect sense. My great-uncle had died in 1914, and his only son was killed at Passchendaele in 1917. No surprise that his widow decided, after the First World War, to keep the Porthmadog home where she had spent all her married life, and to sell this Cheshire house which, though part of their estate, had hardly ever been occupied by Cassons.

Perhaps the most exciting day was when three of us were guided round what had once been the Casson slate quarry. Some time before, I had written to an industrial historian, author of several books about the Welsh quarries, asking how I could visit it. 'As regards visiting Diffwys', he wrote back, ' it is owned by . . . Llechwedd Quarry, but in these Health and Safety days, no-one is going to give you permission. I cannot possibly suggest that you trespass, but were I to do so . . .'. He then gave me clear directions, but the fear of falling into a crevasse held me back, and I thought I must set aside that ambition. And then I was introduced to someone whose partner was the marketing director at Llechwedd. It took only a couple of phone-calls for him to arrange what turned out to be a memorable visit. We were introduced to Errol, one of only two quarriers still employed there. We jumped into his 4 x 4 and he set off across bumpy trails, slopes of slate rising up on either side. I soon lost my sense of direction, but after ten minutes or so, we arrived at the slate face that had once been part of the gorge owned by my great-great-great grandfather and his brother. Of course, we were looking at terraces that had been worked for decades *after* the Cassons sold their quarry, and much imagination was needed to envisage how it had been for them, especially in the early days, when they had the slate carried down to the road on the backs of donkeys and ponies. We spent a long time in the shed where, for years, Errol had cut slate, until it became too uneconomical. Now, most of Llechwedd is given over to a visitors' tour and to zipwire trips. But he was optimistic that there was still slate to be worked. A small quarrying enterprise has since started up, though whether it is in those Diffwys veins first opened up by two Casson brothers in 1800, I have yet to discover.

Much of family history research can now be carried out online. But by far the most interesting part is through meeting new people and seeing new places.

Diana Devlin *read English at Cambridge University and was a Fulbright Scholar at the University of Minnesota, from where she holds a Doctorate in Theatre Arts. She has spent most of her career in the theatre, primarily as a teacher, director and deviser of plays for many generations of students in the UK and USA. Three years ago, she retired after twenty years teaching at the Guildhall School of Music & Drama.*

She has been closely involved with Shakespeare's Globe on Bankside for over forty years, and is now Deputy Chair of its Council. In the 1980s she published a well-received biography of her grandfather, an actor, director and manager: A Speaking Part: Lewis Casson and the Theatre of his Time (Hodder & Stoughton, 1982). She is now well embarked on a biography of his family, who came from the Lake District to North Wales in 1800 and stayed for 150 years.

SUSIE GUTCH

It's hard to believe it's five years since the Faber course ended. I had intended to produce the story of my mother's life for her 91st birthday, and she is now 96! I have written most of it as a first draft, but now comes the hard task of the rewriting and editing process.

During this time, the regular group meetings have been a great source of support and advice. Having met through the course, we realised we share the same challenges in our writing, which can be a lonely activity. In the meetings we are able to offer pieces for discussion, air individual problems and offer suggestions in a friendly and supportive atmosphere. We can set ourselves goals, discuss progress and offer encouragement as well as sharing ideas about research, relevant authors and further courses.

Two authors whom I have found particularly relevant to my writing are Penelope Lively and Michael Holroyd. In her memoir, *Ammonites and Leaping Fish*, Lively discusses the difference between fiction and memoir writing. When writing family history we are dealing with the scope of our ancestors' lives from birth to death, as well as trying to create a structure for all that happened in between. Most lives do not follow an orderly progression and so much happens because of events outside our control – war, illness, death, the need for work and financial security, etc. There may be periods when there is very little information, and the writer may have to make suggestions as to what occurred.

The fiction author has the freedom to structure the plot, to provide a meaningful development for the characters and some sort of satisfactory conclusion to the story. When writing family history, however, use has to be made of information gained through research and where possible by interviewing family members. Then we are dependent on their memories, which are not always consistent or reliable. We have to create a structure from all these different elements.

Apart from being a well-known biographer, Michael Holroyd has written an autobiography and a family memoir. *A Dog's Life* is the fictionalised account of his childhood in the household of his eccentric grandparents. He observed accurately the humour and pathos of the humdrum lives of the family. The humour lies in the intimate portrayal of each character and the minutely described period detail. At the same time, the author is not unsympathetic to the pathos of their situation. In a post-script, Holroyd tells how his father hated the book, and believing that the characters would be easily identifiable, threatened legal action if publication went ahead. Holroyd had had difficulties with threatened litigation with previous biographies he had undertaken, and was used to trying to navigate the problems of an author revealing truths that could hurt the friends and family as well as damage the reputation of his subject.

This is relevant to writing family history as some matters may have been kept secret for years, for what were considered good reasons at the time. Holroyd believes it is important to maintain the truth, in so far as it can be ascertained. The author goes on to analyse the difference between creative fiction as a work of the imagination and what he describes as 'the recreative chronicle of non-fiction.' He does not believe that biographers should be restricted to proven facts, but must also take into account their subjects' 'fantasies, lies, dreams, delusions and contradictions. They must not invent, but they may speculate.' This widens the scope of family historians beyond the bare bones of the 'facts' we can glean about our subjects' lives. Holroyd also points out that biographies need not end with a death – a life story may be told backwards or concentrate on the most interesting parts of a person's life. These are helpful pointers as to how to structure a family history, as well as how to tackle difficult or painful topics when they arise.

Once our *Writing Family History* blog website was set up, I learned how to post monthly pieces and put up photos – both new challenges for me. This was a useful experience in writing a short piece to a deadline on a regular basis and also produced some interesting responses from long-lost members of the family. It was a good way to keep in touch with what the other members of the group were researching and writing about too, between meetings.

I have enjoyed doing the research on my mother's family and the historic context of the late nineteenth and twentieth centuries in Europe and the UK, and this has increased my understanding of the impact of the two World Wars on her life. This has led to much fascinating background reading ranging from Egypt in the early 1900s and Gallipoli in 1915, to the North African campaign in the Second World War and life on the Isle of Wight for civilians in the 1940s.

Through attending various 'Who Do You Think You Are?' events at Olympia I contacted Jayne Shrimpton, the costume and photography expert, whose professional help enabled me to date a number of family photos and miniatures and provided much interesting background information.

In the same way, I was able to contact a professional editor who is advising me how to prepare text and photos for private publication, which is the route I intend to go down having decided to produce a few copies for family and friends only.

The Faber course provided much practical help about research sources, for example The National Archives, the Wellcome Foundation and the Society of Gencalogists, as well as introducing relevant authors and discussing different ways of approaching writing family history. I have subsequently attended a few day courses, but in the end you just have to keep writing, get over the fear of failure and keep reminding yourself of why you wanted to write in the first place. In my case, it was to tell the younger generation about my mother's life and their family history – to put names to the faces in the old photographs and to relate the family stories which otherwise would be lost and forgotten.

---

*Since **Susie Gutch** completed the Faber course in 2011, her husband has retired and they have left their home of 37 years and moved from London to the Isle of Wight. A third grandchild was born 18 months ago, and they find themselves happily involved in childcare once again (on an occasional basis). Susie's mother, Peggy, has just celebrated her 96th birthday – an incentive for Susie to hurry up and finish the book! Peggy has eight great-grandchildren, and it is for them that Susie wishes to write about her life and family history, hoping that the 5th anniversary will spur her on to complete the task.*

MARGARET MCALPINE

Why is my draft still only 95% finished? Do many of us get stuck at the final hurdle? I stopped editing the text over a year ago but outstanding are the commissioning of some local maps and agreement on the copyright of visual material taken from public and private archives. Hopefully my 70,000-word story will be of interest to local studies libraries in Yorkshire. It has turned out part memoir, part PhD without the supervisor and academic oversight. I am nervous of looking an ignorant prat – even if only in the context of local studies.

This was not what I envisaged when I began the research and writing five years ago. My attempt to fictionalise the story was reluctantly abandoned early on. I imagined some ancestors might be important – well, they were but only in their local village of Gomersal in the West Riding of Yorkshire. I had not anticipated what an enormous pleasure the research and discoveries would be. I joked with my family that the prospect of spending a day in an archive was so exciting. They thought I was mad. Chance contacts in Yorkshire and from Ancestry have been invaluable, as well as detailed searches in specialist archives.

From the beginning I decided to focus solely on one branch of my family – the paternal wool mill- owning ancestors who stayed in one place for several centuries and were wealthy enough to leave Wills and feature in Land Tax Records and Deeds libraries.

How and where to end the story is another dilemma. The beginning was not difficult – early eighteenth century - because that is the furthest back I can trace my ancestors but the ending was less clear-cut. While my family lost ownership of Gomersal Mills after the disastrous fire in 1913, the business itself survived under other owners for another 80 years under its original name of Thomas Burnley & Sons at Gomersal Mills. This story deserved to be related until the mill's final demise even though my family no longer had any connection with it. Companies' House is efficient and quick, if expensive, in supplying information and I benefited greatly by access to the Gaunt family private archive.

This short piece tells the story of the family mill's recovery after the major fire in 1913 through to its ultimate demise in the 1990s. It survived longer than many others but finally failed as part of the decline in British manufacturing. My family were not involved in this phase but the mill is central to my story in its own right.

*****

Billy Gaunt, who had bought and rebuilt the mill after the disastrous fire in 1913, died in 1942. His younger son, Derrick Gaunt decided to retain only the former Edwin Woodhouse mill, Sunny Bank - five others, including the Burnley one, were offered for sale to raise some much needed working capital. In 1944 the London and Yorkshire Trust, a private finance company, bought them from West Riding Worsted and Woollen Mills Ltd as a package for a sum rumoured to be in excess of £1 million. Thomas Burnley & Sons Ltd continued to be managed by the Shelton family – three generations of them would work there – proprietors in all but ownership.

Its share capital was increased to £0.5 million in 1949 and in 1950 it acquired Nellroyd Mills, Cleckheaton. The share capital was further increased to £700,000 in 1953. Although wartime restrictions had been dismantled a far more serious threat was about to emerge. Rayon had been the first synthetic fibre to be manufactured commercially in 1911, followed by nylon in 1939. By the mid-1950s a new fibre, acrylic, was widely used in fashion garments and household furnishings. It was versatile, cheap, easily dyed and washed and immune to the moths and mildew that affected wool. It also blended well with traditional fibres like cotton and wool, to make goods that shared the merits of both types of fibre. Polyester came along shortly thereafter. Together with fierce competition from production in cheaper foreign countries and punitive barriers to the import of British goods the very survival of wool textile manufacturing began to look threatened.

In 1969 Thomas Burnley & Sons Ltd became a subsidiary of a huge multinational organisation and at last part of a public company, Coats Patons. That year its Memorandum and Articles of Association were amended to permit it to manufacture and trade in multiple fibres – synthetics had a big competitive advantage over wool on account of their cheapness. From now on, although the company retained its status as a wholly owned subsidiary, due to the integration of operations and acquisition and disposal of assets within the parent group it becomes impossible to make meaningful comparisons with the original business. One thing is certain however, margins were under huge pressure due to factors beyond the company's control.

The next two decades would be a challenging time for British manufacturing in general, and textiles in particular. At its peak in the 1970s Thomas Burnley employed 2,500 workers (not all at Gomersal) some of them bussed in from South Yorkshire, making it a very large operation. Turnover continued to increase from £14 million in 1972 to £27 million in 1979 but profits fluctuated wildly, from around £0.5 million in the better years to a miserable £32,000 in 1978 and a loss of £103,000 in 1979. Despite efforts to embrace the new fibres, by 1979 the future looked ominous, not only for Thomas Burnley & Sons but for the entire industry. Edward Lyons, MP for Bradford West, raised the matter in Parliament in December of that year.

> *I make no apology for being responsible for another debate on textiles, but it is the first one for some time intended to spotlight the problems of the industry in West Yorkshire. There is no alternative for West Yorkshire Members of Parliament but to stress continually to the Government and the civil servants that we cannot allow our area to become depopulated, deprived and a wasteland because of the sickness or death of the textile industry.*

Against this gloomy background Thomas Burnley & Sons did its utmost to modernise, compete and survive. Investment of £10 million in total had been made at mills in Yorkshire and Northern Ireland (Ambler at Ballyclare). They claimed to be Britain's largest suppliers of worsted-spun yarn to the knitting industry, producing six million kilograms of acrylic-dyed years at their mill at Ballyclare in Northern Ireland. There were some peak years in the 1980s when profits of several million pounds were reported, one of the best being 1987 which produced an operating profit of £4 million on a turnover of £54.9 million. The Chairman reported that the favourable trading conditions were set to continue in the short term. A swift decline then set in. By 1989 the outlook was poor.

In 1986 Coats Patons was itself taken over by Vantona Viyella. The bid offer was worth about £714 million and the new company became Coats Viyella Plc. From now on the performance of Thomas Burnley & Sons Ltd is opaque with much reorganisation and transfer of assets and operations across subsidiary companies and disposals. Whatever the strategic intention behind it all, the outcome spelt the end for the old family firm. The cost of a corporate restructure showed up in the results for 1990, with a £1 million loss on a turnover of £40 million, against an extraordinary item of £5.4 million charge for closure and reorganisation.

By 1992 employee numbers had slipped to 500 and there was a loss of nearly £1 million on a turnover of £32 million. The following year, 1993, 250 jobs were lost when the spinning department closed and by 1994 the company had ceased trading. In 1995 Thomas Burnley & Sons' assets were bought by IPT in a deal worth £89.4 million who sold on various parts to others. Later the Gomersal site was cleared of all its other manufacturing and sold to developers for housing.

Today the landscape of the West Riding is dominated by its textile past. Mills have been converted to housing or other industrial uses; some lie empty and semi-derelict. Those of significant architectural merit, such as Salts at Saltaire or Dean Clough in Halifax, have been renovated and preserved for a mix of cultural, business, commercial, residential and leisure use. Gomersal Mills, much altered in the 1870s and rebuilt after the fire in 1913, could claim neither historical significance nor architectural merit. An archaeological excavation found little evidence of the original eighteenth-century Cloth Hall building. The enormous 180 foot chimney, a Spen Valley landmark, was one of the last structures to be demolished in June 2004 by the house builders, Persimmon. It had become unsafe. The Burnley family firm still exists on the register at Companies' House as a dormant company wholly owned by Coats plc. It has not traded since 1994. A token road name sign is its only physical memorial.

What would Victorian Thomas Burnley (1797-1863) have made of all this? Pragmatic and unsentimental he had already diversified his investments into railway stock, gas supply and commercial property by the time of his death. I doubt he would feel a sense of loss and nor indeed do I – only a strong rapport with God's Own County.

Margaret McAlpine, *a history graduate, has always wanted to write more creatively than her various public service jobs allowed. Her interest in family history began with her grandmother's stories of lost wealth and status but had been laid aside for many years, awaiting time and perhaps that indispensable tool, the internet. If her family memoir, which is nearing completion, provides readers with only a fraction of the pleasure she has had in researching and writing it, it will still replay her debt to that community – scholars, authors and publishers – who have made history so relevant and enjoyable for us all today.*

TRACEY MESSENGER

Anniversaries invariably cause us both to look back to the event which they mark, and forwards. How many more such anniversaries will we see?

We have taken the opportunity of the occasion of the fifth anniversary of the end of our writing course to review our progress. Where are we now? And where do we go from here?

Some of us are nearing completion of our projects; others are still wrestling with the perennial problem of structure, or pursuing that elusive missing fact that will prove to be the key to all mysteries. For others, myself included, there is the dilemma of how to break the news to our relatives that we've been secretly writing about them for five years.

As with all non-fiction writing projects, there is a great deal of plodding involved: diligent searching through census returns; hours spent in the British Library getting backache as you attempt to speed read several years' worth of local newspapers in one go (not advisable– thankfully the cafe has a loyalty card). And all for the thrill of tracking down that one fact that will either prove a cherished hypothesis, or blow it out of the water entirely.

I've had a number of such 'Aha!' moments that bring us family history geeks such joy. But the reason we history hounds keep searching is more than the enjoyment and satisfaction of finding that elusive fact. At the risk of sounding portentous, it's something to do with finding out the truth.

When you start researching family history there are a couple of golden rules:

- Mine your remaining relatives for as much information as they are willing to give.
- Treat what they say with a pinch of salt ...

My project is about my grandmother's family and as she was one of 13 children, 12 of whom lived to adulthood, there is a huge extended clan. One of the stories passed down through relatives concerns my great-grandfather, Tom Robinson, the protagonist of the first part of my book. It was said that one of his children, Mary Agnes, had died as the result of a compulsory smallpox vaccination and Tom had gone to court to secure an exemption from the vaccination for subsequent children. It's a colourful and attractive story, containing both pathos at the death of a child and heroism, as Tom battled the authorities to protect his brood. I looked forward to including this incident in my book as an example of Tom's stubborn and determined character (for non-fiction writers must bring characters alive on the page too).

But was it true? Off I went to investigate whether there were records held locally of those who had applied to have their children exempted from the compulsory smallpox vaccination programme. Sadly, such records (from the early 1900s) did not survive. It is possible that Tom may have had to appear before the local Quarter Sessions: but as the county archivist advised me that these vast records were un-indexed, I decided against going down that route.

In the meantime, other records had made me wonder whether the smallpox story might not be entirely accurate. A local resident gave me access to the log book for the village school, in which the teachers not only recorded attendance but reasons for absence, e.g. weather conditions, a Band of Hope outing – or illness. From this log book I discovered that in the spring of 1908, just before Mary Agnes Robinson died, whooping cough was rife in the village.

Of course I had neglected the easiest way to find out whether the smallpox story was true: obtaining a copy of Mary Agnes's death certificate from the General Record Office. For family historians, the arrival of an envelope from the GRO is a cause of great excitement (tasteless though this may seem: these are after all the records of the births, marriages and deaths of real people). And there it was in black and white: 'Mary Agnes Robinson, female, 10 months'. Cause of death: 'Bronchitis & Whooping Cough, 10 days', informant 'T.Robinson, father, present at the death'. It was those final few words that undid me: I had pinned down a fact and solved a mystery, but they were real people who had witnessed before their eyes the death of their ten-month old child. I wept for these great-grandparents I'd never met.

There may have been some truth in the story. Perhaps it concerned another child. But those who may have been able to shed light on this are no longer around and the family historian must do her best to make a judgement on the known facts.

Tracking down records has disproved other family myths too, such as, 'your grandfather never stuck at anything'. The fact that he voluntarily joined the army at 19 and travelled to Germany, India and Burma, where he took part in quashing the Burma Rebellion of the early 1930s, before being invalided out of the forces, would seem to belie this assessment of his character.

And then there are our own romantic hypotheses about why an event may have happened. Much of my book is about the Methodism within my grandmother's family, but there are Roman Catholic ancestors in there too, on my grandfather's side. As he was born in Liverpool, I speculated excitedly about an Irish great-grandmother. She would have brought a bit of exotic colour into my otherwise solidly Cumbrian ancestry. But, somewhat disappointingly, she proved to be as Cumbrian as the rest. And the Roman Catholicism did not appear to come from her side.

For reasons I don't entirely understand myself, I became somewhat obsessed with finding out where it *had* come from. Until Irish immigration increased in the Victorian period, after the Reformation Roman Catholicism only really survived in north-west England through the influence of a few landed families. One such family was the Howards, related to the Dukes of Norfolk, who had married into the Dacres of Cumberland. They held estates in the county at Greystoke, Naworth and Corby castles. Finding out that my grandfather's family had roots in Matterdale, on the fringes of Ullswater, and once part of the Greystoke estate, I thought I'd found the link. Perhaps my family had worked as retainers for the Howards and, like others, had taken on their faith?

But again, further research uncovered facts that dispelled this romantic speculation: the Greystoke Howards converted to Anglicanism in the 1830s, before my great-great-grandfather was born. Moreover, I've subsequently discovered that my great-great-grandparents were married in the Anglican parish church in Penrith, had their first child baptised there and then performed a volte face by having all their subsequent children baptised as Roman Catholics. I think a road to Damascus-style conversion was unlikely: it may be that they wanted their children to get into the Roman Catholic school closest to their home. They may have been Roman Catholics of convenience rather than conviction. How very unromantic!

My adventures in family history over the last five years have shown that those stories handed down over generations through families should be received with gladness and gratitude but handled circumspectly. As historians, we owe it to our ancestors to find out, as far as we can, the truth of the matter. They still may not recognise the accounts we have written of their lives and times (and I think my grandmother may have been horrified by my speculations on what she might have thought or felt at any given time). But in striving to find out what really happened, I seek to honour those who have gone before, whose stories would otherwise be lost to posterity.

Tracey Messenger *is a Commissioning Editor working in religious publishing and spends her days editing the work of others. Whether this is helpful in writing and completing her own project remains to be seen. She has had a longstanding interest in what makes people tick, which has led to studies in English literature, history, theology and psychology of religion. Her project, sparked by her grandmother's stories about her strict Methodist father, is a religious history of her family spanning the twentieth century. She is regularly distracted from this task by Peggy, a three-year-old miniature schnauzer.*

BARBARA SELBY

When I started thinking about researching and then writing about my family stories all those years ago I was still working full-time. I thought of the Faber Course in terms of providing me with skills for a retirement hobby but it has led to so much more. Most importantly it led to a group of friends who continue to provide me with the inspiration and encouragement to stick with my writing.

My first research, helped by a breakthrough provided by Annie, one of the other Faber students, concentrated on finding the story behind objects passed down in a number of tin boxes and in identifying the artist who painted the pictures I had inherited. This part of my mother's family had migrated to America and theirs felt like the most romantic story my family had to tell. I even wrote about their journey for our first anthology. But romantic though the story is, and it is one I need to tell properly sometime, it is no longer the story I am currently writing.

The combination of too many mysteries and too little hard information diverted me onto what seemed an easier path: that is the other side of my mother's family, a Yorkshire family of clothiers from whom emerged my great-grandfather, an engineer, writer and inventor. Whereas my American family had romance and mystery, my Yorkshire family had photograph albums of refuse destructor plants and books on cost accounting. Less romance, so I thought, but a simpler story to tell with more evidence available to build on.

Apart from the longer piece I wrote for the anthology, my initial forays into the writing world were all short pieces for our blog. In terms of acquiring skills for retirement I can now write a blog, analyse its performance and use social media; all to my surprise and often my great delight (and occasional frustration!). But there is a world of difference between the 500-word sound bite of a blog and writing even a chapter in someone's life. A blog can be just one idea, one object or incident described and briefly commented on, a few good images and maybe an apt quotation and then post it and be done.

The curse of retirement for me is the removal of any structure to the day, week, month, even the year. I have always known I needed to work to deadlines and organising my writing and research into the spaces left by a relatively demanding professional life was somehow easier than finding I had 'all the time in the world'. All the time in the world that is, to follow clues to more random fragments down the labyrinthine paths of the web. Web is such an appropriate name: how it entices and entraps until hours have gone by and I am still hunched over my computer, legs crossed and desperate for something to eat and drink but unable to break free until I have nailed a completely obscure fact about someone who crossed great-grandfather's path once, possibly. Who but me could possibly be interested in, for example, William Deeble Ferguson who left a Belfast foundry as great-grandfather arrived. But he was, exciting fact alert, also a draper's son. Perhaps it was his name that drew me in – after all, what's not to like about an engineer called Deeble? And there I go again – another footnote that says more about my love of obscure facts than anything revealing about great-grandfather's life.

I knew I needed to build on the initial guidance from our Faber course and force myself into a routine if I was ever to have more than a series of disconnected blogs and so I booked myself onto another course. This time it can with a glowing recommendation from Diana, another Writing Family History group friend. So last September I started the *Guardian* 'Writing the New Biography' course. A move away from family history you might think, but not so far in reality. My biography subject still is that same great-grandfather who left behind the photo albums of refuse destructors, but I now see him as so much more. The *Guardian* course has taught me to see him in the context of his family's values – non-conformist and Liberal, and of his times – the beginning of the end of the Victorian love affair with engineering.

But also his story is telling me about myself, about how much of our present is rooted in our family's past. I can see the threads of politics and religion and engineering being woven together into a new pattern – a logical, mathematical progression. From Methodist to Congregationalist to Atheist and Humanist; from Whig to Liberal and onto schisms of the centre and radical left and from the broad breadth of the general Victorian Engineer at his drawing board to the narrow specialist engineer at her computer.

So now to the details. My project is the life and times of Alfred John Liversedge (AJL), engineer and inventor, born in Huddersfield in 1854.

This is a 'cradle-to-grave' biography told from a third-person point of view. At first I put myself in the story and used both the first person and present tense but feedback I received indicated that this did not really work. I now feel more comfortable creating a slight distance from my subject and consider that this creates a professional style more suited to the project.

I begin with AJL's family background, taking the family back to his grandparents at the start of the nineteenth century. Here I hope to give a sense of the position the family occupied in society and their strong non-conformist and liberal traditions. I am learning how to draw conclusions from the limited evidence I have, particularly about his father's fortunes. This is especially hard for someone like me, someone used professionally to analysing hard data to arrive at firm conclusions.

An element of my book will be the various inventions AJL patented throughout his life. However I realised that inserting these into the main book would result in these either being skimped and trivialised or, if treated in enough detail, would disrupt the narrative. Reading Kathryn Hughes' biography of Mrs Beeton, I was impressed with her use of 'interludes' between the chapters to present information from her subject's *Book of Household Management*. I intend to treat AJL's inventions in this way heading them, 'Innovation and Invention'. As there are no examples from AJL until the 1880s, the first two are inventions by those who would have influenced him. The third will be his own patent for improvements to the safe-lamp.

So far I have three chapters and two-and-a-half interludes and although I know they need a lot more work, I do feel that at last I am making progress. Although my project, along with my life, has changed significantly since I took my first step with the writing family history course, I know I would not have got even this far without the support of the group that grew from that. Thank you.

Barbara Selby *was born in the retirement resort of Bexhill-on-Sea in the year tea rationing ended and The Mousetrap began its record-breaking run. She studied maths and more maths leading to a degree in Civil Engineering from Leeds University. After working for many years in local government, she retired from her final post as Head of Transport Planning on the last day of 2011. She still lives in London where she spends her days in her club, The Institution of Civil Engineers, at 1 Great George Street drinking coffee, eating the free biscuits and pretending to write.*

VANITA SHARMA

Researching and writing about your family history is a very personal and often solitary activity. By its very nature, you may assume that it's something that only your family will want to know about. If you're lucky, as you piece together the fragments of your family's past, relatives will rally round to contribute what they know and will eagerly wait to see the finished results of your research. But along the way you will more than likely discover that not everyone will be so keen to explore the family's past. Some family members simply won't be interested, while others may be keen to prevent long-buried secrets being dug up. As you delve deeper, you may also find yourself facing difficult moral quandaries about what do with the stories you uncover.

I've experienced all of this during my own search to learn about my family history. But over the last five years, I've been lucky to have our Writing Family History Group as an invaluable support base. We've shared and listened to each other's stories, provided ideas on new research angles, questions and sources, and encouraged each other at times when we've felt like giving up. The group has also often been a sounding board for us to discuss our new discoveries, oftentimes ahead of sharing them with our own families.

As the years have passed, I've become as invested in learning more about everyone else's stories, as much as my own. Our family stories bridge different generations, varied historical periods and multiple geographies, but there are many common themes in the stories we've discovered. We've found both female and male ancestors who had to defy social and familial barriers and expectations to build the lives they wanted; we've discovered how our families have lost and gained money; as well as unearthing the truth behind family feuds, secrets and tragedies. We've learned about how religious attitudes in our families have changed and found out how our families were affected by the industrial revolution, by colonialism and by wars in different parts of the world. Our stories have given us unique glimpses into how major historical events have shaped the lives of ordinary families like our's. And, as we've traced how our ancestors migrated during their lifetimes and over generations, some of us have also uncovered that the roots of our families are much more widespread than we initially thought.

I was born in England to Indian parents and my own interest in learning more about my family history began when I discovered that my grandfather was born in a village that is now part of Pakistan. This eventually led me to travel across India and Pakistan to meet families devastated by the 1947 Partition which divided British India and created Pakistan. 14.5 million people were uprooted by Partition – Hindus and Sikhs fled to the reduced India and Muslims escaped to the new Pakistan. At least half a million people were killed in a few months, as neighbour turned on neighbour. Some estimates place the death toll nearer 2 million. My book features the stories of families from both sides who were affected by Partition, as well as telling the story of my search to find out more about my own family history in India and Pakistan.

I'm currently putting the finishing touches on my manuscript and I could not have reached this far without the support of our group. They have inspired me with their own searches and stories, and encouraged me to keep going at many moments when I may have given up, for which I am deeply grateful. Although my book is nearing completion, my search to learn more about my family history isn't over and I look forward to many more of our gatherings over the coming years.

Vanita Sharma *read Modern History and English Literature at the University of Oxford, where she earned B.A., M.St. and D.Phil. degrees. She has taught South Asian History at the University of Oxford; at the School of Oriental and African Studies (SOAS), London; and at the Lahore University of Management Sciences (LUMS), Pakistan. She was awarded a Scholar of Peace Fellowship by the Dalai Lama Foundation and has been involved in a number of peace initiatives between India and Pakistan. She currently works as a Communications Consultant.*

PATRIZIA SORGIOVANNI

BACKGROUND

My project is about my great grandmother and her daughters (there were seven sisters). It is based in the 1950s, in a small village in southern Italy. There is a murder in the family. One of the sisters killed her sister's husband. There is so much drama that the story practically writes itself.

Aside from the Faber group, my parents, my 'twin' cousin Sandie (our ages are 6 months apart), and the actor Bill Nighy (who I met in a café and happened to talk to about the project!), no one knows I am writing the book. My research has been done incognito. Why, you may ask? Many of the main characters are still alive. Secrecy and gossip hold equal importance for my grandmother and her sisters. As long as they think they are sharing gossip with me, they are happy to share information. I am afraid that if they knew I was writing a book, the sweet lovely details of their lives – both the beautiful and harrowing – will be locked up in the secrecy safe of their minds.

I should mention that the family members I'm writing about all live in Italy, and not many of them speak English. There is a chance I could publish the book and they would never find out.

In this piece, I reflect on the five years I've spent writing their story.

STAGE ONE: EXCITEMENT - JUNE 2012 – AUGUST 2012

We had just finished the Faber Academy Writing Family History course. We had written an anthology of our stories, endorsed by Faber Academy. We even had a book launch. Afterwards, an agent reached out and said she was interested in my story. It wasn't even the murder part that she liked, but the way I described one of the scenes. She actually liked my writing!

I was on top of the world – *I will be a famous author, my book will be made into a movie. Tourist will flock to the village which I write about and revive it.*

I created a blog to help keep the group together and to keep me writing. As a group we agreed to meet once per month to keep each other motivated. My parents became my allies in the secret mission to get information. My 'twin' cousin was ecstatic. My dear friends were very supportive. All was going according to plan.

Soon I would leave my job and be a full time writer – I could even write other people's stories! Not just about the women in my family, about other women. Yes, I shall pursue this as a profession!

Emotions: excitement, ecstatic, fun, flow (woo hoo!)

STAGE TWO: DEPRESSION – AUGUST 2012 – APRIL 2013

I lost a big work contract. I broke up with my boyfriend. Life changed, and so did my energy for the book. I spent three weeks in the Italian village where the story is set, hoping to get inspiration, but writing didn't happen. I spent more time setting up my little writing space in the attic of the old house that my mother inherited, than in actually writing. Resigning myself to writer's block, I focused on collecting stories.

My favourite discovery was learning about the professional mourners. Women were hired to cry and make a dramatic scene at funerals, so the family didn't have to. Mourning was outsourced. (Apparently a tradition dating back to the Phoenicians).

When I got back from Italy, the depression took over a bit more. I was still managing the blog, but not writing any posts, for fear my cousins who speak English would find it. What once was a project that brought me much joy became a guilt-laden burden on my shoulders.

Emotions: Sad, down, lethargy, apathy, paranoia

STAGE THREE: A SPARK OF ENERGY - APRIL 2013 - JULY 2013

In the spring of 2013, I found energy to search for and attend two Urban Writing Retreats. In just those two days (three weeks apart) I made significant progress on my project. I managed to organize my research and create a detailed outline. I created a timeline of all the characters in the book, their ages and locations for each of the book's sections to ensure continuity. My dad excitedly proofed the timeline, and filled in the blanks. I once again loved immersing myself into photographs and the stories, imagining what life was like for my great grandmother. I began transcribing the interviews and heard new things I hadn't picked up the first time.

Maybe I need this space and time to write about things in a new way. It was all meant to be. All is fine. I am now ready to finish the manuscript.

I reached out to the agent to remind her of her interest in my project.

Her reply:'Yes, do send us something when you're ready whether, whenever that may be. And don't worry - we understand that most authors have to fit it into the day job somehow.' What a relief! I hadn't missed my chance. And a new agent got in touch! She wanted to see a manuscript. Now I had two agents interested in the story. I had renewed energy. *The project is back on. This is my time.*

I got the nerve to visit and interview the aunt who committed the crime. Much to my surprise she openly discussed life in jail and kept referring to what happened as 'La disgrazia' – the unfortunate event. As if it just 'happened'. She openly shared more than I expected. She seemed happy that someone had an interest in her life.

Emotions: hope, fear, anxiety that this feeling will not last.

STAGE FOUR: LETTING GO - AUGUST 2013 – MAY 2015

Life once again got in the way of the book. Work picked up, I moved to a new flat, I was dating again, I had knee surgery.

The book was on my mind, but my willingness to work on it was lost. I felt defeated.

Maybe I should just let go of the project. But I couldn't do it. I knew it was something I had to finish. If I wasn't going to work on it actively, I could do more research before anyone else died. I decided that the bare minimum was to keep collecting stories. On every trip to Italy, I scanned more photos; I sat with old ladies; I listened and recorded them.

Things I (or others) tried to help me write:
- I went to healers and palm readers
- Writing commitments with Vanita and Tracey and Susie
- Accountability 'dream project' support groups
- Writing weekends at friends
- Dating rich men in the hope they would offer to pay for my life for a few months while I wrote
- Friends told me to create the book cover – to get inspired
- Endless telling-offs from Sandie

Nothing worked. Sandie stopped talking to me. My dad asked, 'Whatever happened with the book?' I decided to let go. *It will happen when/if it is meant to.*

Emotions: Guilt, shame, anger, desperation, defeat

STAGE FIVE - ACCEPTANCE – 6TH JUNE 2015 - PRESENT

June 2015 was another turning point. Work was going well. I loved my home. I was semi-dating someone I liked. I heard that some people take 10 years to write their book. This gave me hope to look at my writing again.

One afternoon, my friend Denise and I devoted an undisturbed three hours to our projects. We agreed to let go of shame, and just reconnect with our writing. Acceptance was the word we used. In those three hours I wrote and wrote and wrote! I could see the village and my great grand-mother's life. It was as if she was whispering in my ear.

Those three hours were enough to remind me how much I loved writing about these women. The writing continued every day for the next 10 days. My routine was an hour a day, first thing in the morning. I began sending pieces to Sandie and others who were interested. Feedback was 'I want more!'

A month later the Faber group had a meeting to decide whether or not to continue meeting as a group. Panic struck. *We can't stop meeting!* It showed me the importance of putting energy into what I love. My attendance had been low, but I didn't want the group to dismantle. I had to rearrange my priorities, to make the book and the group more of a priority in my life.

Today work is busy but I have made time to meet with a writing buddy once a week. I accept I will finish my project when I finish it. I am devoted to the group – although my attendance could be better. I really value connecting with such well-read, supportive and inspiring women every month. I don't want that to end. I don't want the writing to end.

Emotions: Calm, happy, inspired

The moral of the story – it is so easy to let life get in the way of doing what I love. It takes a conscious effort not to let it. I'm still learning.

A Canadian of Italian origin, **Patrizia Sorgiovanni's** *fascination with her family history began at the age of 12. On summer holiday in southern Italy, she would ask her grandmother endless questions about life growing up in the village. An animated storyteller, her grandmother would happily divulge detailed, colourful answers, along with some interesting family secrets.*

In 2001, driven by a deep interest in her family history, Patrizia moved to Italy to reconnect with her family. Three years later, her job transferred her to London, but she continually makes trips to the village of her ancestors to capture the way of life that is slowly dying.

Patrizia's project focuses on the life of her great grandmother, Marina. The story is about Marina's life between the 1940s and the 1960s, providing a glimpse into a vanishing lifestyle. The plot is based on the passionate rivalry between headstrong sisters leading to disastrous results.

NICOLA STEVENS

I would describe my writing process over the last five years as a tango dance. I firmly hold my partner – the project – our arms outstretched, pointing the direction forward. With focus and passion, we both purposely take parallel steps to start the dance. My path of research has been sprinkled with surprises; obstacles that require critical pivots, side-steps, sharp head turns and unexpected ankle flicks. Like a tango routine that covers the whole dance floor before coming to its exhilarating end, my research has covered others' lives and periods, gathering facts and myths from family ephemera, quiet archives and chance conversations that strike like lightning. I feel that whether a writing project will only be read within the family circle or will become the next best- seller, it is not an adventure for sissies. Do not despair. Before anyone scuttles off to companies that ghost-write family memoirs I can say that after a bit of self-discovery everyone has the potential to write their own.

Although I joined the Faber Academy Writing Family History course I have not been writing about my own family but a Flemish artist, Joseph van Heacken (Aken), and his family. They left their Antwerp home in the embattled Spanish Netherlands (now Belgium) and came to England around 1720, the year of the first major financial crisis as the South Sea Bubble burst. The first bald facts I gleaned from art dictionaries captured my heart and mind. The Faber Academy course felt a good way to create the habit of focus and daily writing rather than just work commitments, family and social necessities. In autumn 2011 I was due to start a Masters degree in *Writing Narrative Non-Fiction* at City University, London, as I wanted to publish this project.

'How's Joe coming along?', friends would ask as I struggled to make sense of research sources which included official family documents, Joe's friends' sketchy memories and second-hand reports in gossipy letters. Sometimes there are three different versions of the same event and I found nine variations of the family name, from 'van Heacken' to 'van Aken'. Unexpected information changed the emphasis of their story.

Brothers became cousins, unknown fathers suddenly appeared in London to die, their possessions auctioned by their widows. As one of my course colleagues searched through Chancery Court Rolls in The National Archives, Kew[1] for her own project, she found a record of a van Heacken family financial dispute in the 1770s. Part of the Plaintiff's evidence included a Flemish van Heacken family tree. That was an exhilarating moment needing a critical pivot and unexpected ankle flick, then a sharp side-step followed after realising the family church in Antwerp and all its records of births, deaths and marriages were destroyed by Napoleon's army in the 1790s. No wonder, then, that I could not find any information on the family during visits to Antwerp, but I would have never thought to search the Chancery Court records, even on a whim.

Sadly, in spite of research surprises, it became apparent that there was not enough information to write a traditional biography of Joe. Instead I decided to use the van Heacken family as a conduit to peek behind the studio door into the business of art in the first half of eighteenth-century London. Artistically the first fifty years of the eighteenth century are usually dismissed as mechanical, rather than innovative; the worst artistic period in British history, some say, dominated by foreigners. Art historians prefer pinpointing later British masters to illustrate artistic genius in the eighteenth century such as portraitists Joshua Reynolds and Thomas Gainsborough or Richard Wilson and John Constable for landscapes.

During one of my slow periods, when I guiltily devoured any book from romance to science fiction instead of writing, a friend sent me a copy of Stephen King's book, *On Writing: A Memoir of the Craft*. I felt exonerated as I read the following quote:

'If you want to be a writer you must do two things above all others: read a lot and write a lot.'

So I was halfway to becoming a real writer, I just needed to increase my daily word count! King's productive schedule was simple. He generated new work in the morning. The afternoons are for naps and letters. Evenings are for:

' …(sic) reading, family, Red Sox games on TV, and any other revisions that just cannot wait.'

I know King is a professional writer but just giving the evening to family? What about his friends?

I flicked through the preceding two months in my diary. It was littered with calls from a friend with a broken arm needing help. I'd had a friend's dog to stay who only 'did her business' on grass which meant endless trips to the park including early in the morning wearing a thick coat to cover nightwear with bed socks in gumboots to keep my feet dry. My eighty-five-year-old uncle collapsed on a trip to London and the least I could do was deliver the daily papers while he languished in hospital. Water had dripped through the bathroom ceiling from the flat above and run down a light fitting in the hallway.

This is my kind of life. I think those interested in their family history have a default switch in their biological or nurtured DNA that makes them the person that family and friends turn to for help. They are the repository of birthdays, family ephemera and ancient relatives' anecdotes. Usually, but not always, these are women and I have spent the last five years with ten of these intrepid females who persevere with their writing projects while their families and friends still call on their time, devoting 30 minutes or an hour each day to write come what may – no sharp head turn needed here. A little often is best. Switch on a timer and disappear into the writing until the buzzer goes.

Like King, the morning is my best writing time. I have devised different ways to find time for co-writing business books depending on the flow of my work or the state of my health. I was diagnosed with M.E. (Myalgic Encephalopathy) three years ago. While working I used to set my first alarm for 5am, fall out of bed, make a cup of tea, stagger to my computer and start typing straight away still wearing my nightie as I followed the list of next writing steps I had made the day before. My second alarm would ring at 7am so I could leave the writing project behind and get ready for my working day. One summer I had breakfast in the local café with a pad of paper and pencil to start my writing morning. When I felt I wanted to type instead of write longhand on the pad I went straight home to type. However I learned that I needed to tidy my flat before I left so that the sight of dirty plates or a pile of washing did not divert me on my return.

Recently I read an article online[2], 'Your Brain Has A "Delete" Button—Here's How To Use It' by Judah Pollack and Olivia Fox Cabane, that highlighted the advantage of regular habits. When we sleep our brains switch on a deleting process called 'synaptic pruning' that identifies connections within the brain that are not being used regularly to make room for new skills and information. It really is a case of 'use it or lose it'.

Since being diagnosed with M.E., I start my day in bed with a pad and pencils. The increased collaboration between libraries, educational and other institutions via the Internet makes remote information easily accessible. World Cat[3] can be used to find out which libraries have the specialist book you may need. Some membership institutions such as the London Library[4] allow readers to use their e-catalogue and Catalyst to read and print texts remotely at home from JSTOR[5] or other collections of printed matter. The British Library only allows information to be seen while on their premises, but you can reserve the books online so they are ready for you when you arrive. The London Metropolitan Archives[6] allows readers to search membership family websites free in its premises. Research first starts by locating the information you need for your project.

My self-discovery meant I needed to identify my best writing time, make realistic immoveable daily writing periods and read anything and everything. I think that whether the writing project is for the family or for general publication, writers need to track their sources but still make their writing more than a list of facts. Then future generations will be able to retrace these steps and the lives of the hardworker or the wastrel will be kept alive long after living memories have died.

Buena suerte with your tango dance.

i *www.nationalarchives.gov.uk/*
ii *www.fastcompany.com/3059634/your-most-productive-self/your-brain-has-a-delete-button-heres-how-to-use-it*
iii *www.worldcat.org/*
iv *www.londonlibrary.co.uk/*
v *www.jstor.org/*
vi *www.cityoflondon.gov.uk/things-to-do/london-metropolitan-archives/Pages/default.aspx*

Nicola Stevens *began a part time MA in Writing Narrative Non-Fiction at City University, London in September 2011. Sadly she was diagnosed with M.E. (Myalgic Encephalopathy) and had to defer her MA twice while giving up working for the foreseeable future. However, Nicola has completed the six taught MA terms and is now writing the van Heacken (Aken) family's story about coming to London as émigrés in 1720 and settled into the English business of art. Nicola continues to discover more paintings by the family as auction houses, libraries, educational and art institutions increase their collaboration through the Internet.*

CLARE TRAVERS

'The end of all our exploring
will be to arrive where we started ...'

From *Little Gidding* by T.S. Eliot

When we put together our anthology a year after the end of the Writing Family History course, we each wrote a synopsis before an extract from our writing project. In mine, I wrote about my elder son Sam's wedding and here we are, five years later, with another wedding in the offing, that of my younger son, Jack. So, we have come full circle via that first wedding, as well as the death of my father and the birth of two granddaughters. As things have turned out, no discernible progress has been made with the plan I had back then to write the story of the early years of our marriage that were spent in Turkey and Africa. Back in 2011 my mother had returned to me the letters I had written during those years abroad and the idea was to read them, edit them and try to write the story behind the letters. As a project it sounds simple and do-able, doesn't it, to re-read letters that you have written and shape them into book form, with an authorial narrative thread running through the whole thing. But, five years on, I am not sure that it is easy at all.

I had another reason for my project: one born out of the terrible sadness of losing our eldest child, Amelia - the little baby we had taken to Africa in 1982 and who had died in 1999. The project, I thought, would be a way of keeping alive the very fact of her being with us all those years ago, somehow crystallizing the experience, making it even more precious. Family memories are 'fragile treasures' as Kate Grenville puts it in her own memoir of her mother, *One Life*, and it only takes one generation to not pass those treasures on and they are gone, a point made poignant for us with Amelia's sudden death. So, the reason to write was there, the material was there – yet somehow I still held off. That point when you have crossed the threshold, when the 'pen gets on the scent' as Virginia

Woolf wrote in *A Writer's Diary*, when the thinking is done and the page awaits a mark still eludes me as a complete narrative. Episodes, incidents, monographs, those I can do. Yet, to me, all that does not amount to a cohesive whole, a first draft in other words. I want that feeling of knowing, just knowing, that what I am writing, or about to write, is right: that it is, in essence, building itself as the words hit the page and, that when that happens, the story will become as much a part of the fabric of the life we had then as the photographs we took and developed ourselves in a darkroom in our house in the bush.

In part, the fact that it remains unwritten in a proper form is down to my lack of faith in the act of my own writing. I am also a reluctant recorder of myself. The very act of re-reading the letters was sometimes difficult and I have yet to read through them all. There is something unsettling about looking back at your young, naïve self. It is much easier to read someone else's letters and draw your own conclusions about them. A sense of doubt lingers that I cannot make those years sing on the page – and I want them to sing, very much.

Whether I am able do that is not actually the whole point. Somewhere along the line I must have wanted to do it. Not just to hand on those 'fragile treasures' alone, but to do it for myself, to recognize that it was an unusual and even courageous thing to do, to go off and live where we did at that time in our lives. Now, thirty-odd years on, finding the confidence to face the blank page and write anything at all feels like an act of courage in itself. So, here we are in 2016 and our anticipated house move has not materialized and, my restless nature tamed for the moment, there really should be no sense of dislocation or disruption to stand between my pen and my project. In fact, that restless nature which took me abroad with a new husband and small children, far from anyone or anything that was familiar, should be the spur that keeps me at it.

When I look back over these five years that we have been together as a group who encourage, support, suggest and listen to one another, I can only hope that we go on for five more years and five more after that, as it is through our interaction that I have learnt most. One of the first things we had to do at Faber was read aloud a piece that we had written. It was when I read mine and everyone seemed to like it, that I realized I could do it, this thing, this idea that I had to record those precious years. The companionship of the group and the ideas that come out of our meetings are two things that writers probably need most, to stave off that sense of isolation that writing by oneself can bring. I'm very lucky to be part of a group of such sympathetic women whose experiences in writing are always worth listening to and learning from.

T.S. Eliot's words keep playing on my mind: the end of all my exploring in the writing of the story does indeed take me back to where I started, both literally and metaphorically. The journey in writing, as in life, has been full of incident and learning, and, after five years, perhaps now I will arrive at the point where the blank page will offer up its possibilities and take me on a deeper journey to its heart.

Since doing the Faber Writing Family History course in 2011, **Clare Travers***'s life has been delightfully enlivened by the arrival in 2014 and 2015, of two granddaughters. That is no excuse, but the story that was inspired by the Writing Family History course has yet to be written. Now, when it is, it will be as much for Emily and Holly (and, hopefully, future grandchildren) as for Clare's own children. A move away from Shropshire in 2016, a long time in the planning, has had to be put on hold. However, as some compensation for that, there is now a sense of being in a more settled place for her writing to take shape.*

KRISTINA TZANEFF

Time. It is given to us before it's taken. In between, it's up to us to make of it what we will. We are writing about time when we write our family histories, preserving them through the written word.

Five years on from the end of our Writing Family History course, it turns out that writing about family is a harder feat than one might expect, one requiring a plan, perseverance and discipline.

My 'plan', fortunately, came from an already established structure which twelve of us initially committed to when the course finished in June, 2011. In addition to teaching us to structure and write our family histories, this class became much more, as a group of us continued in the spirit of what we'd learned over those six months and found a way to keep our learning and network alive. Our monthly meetings at Waterstone's, Piccadilly, on alternating Tuesdays and Saturday mornings would set the tone for me over the next five years.

During these five years our group met and discussed the development of our respective stories, brought in experts to help teach us something about websites and assigned ourselves the task of each blogging bi-monthly. Soon, we had built up a solid digital archive of our respective stories. In the meantime we presented bits of writing to each other for feedback as we were aware of the wonderful tool we had in each other for listening, learning and critiquing. All in all, we found an amazing resource in each other and we valued it as we knew that such a group is difficult to come by and even more difficult to sustain.

The beginning of my five-year writing journey was marked by the passing away of my father, three weeks after I had started the course. My father had been the cornerstone of my research up until that time, taking me back through history and his childhood by the interviews which he granted me. With him, I had a chance to ask all the questions I had in tying people to places and connecting relevant bits of information. When he was gone, I was left to rely on my notes. I came to learn the hard way that information in Eastern Europe, whether historical or current, is not as abundant or nearly as well-organised as that in the west. Records had been lost or data transferred over systems incompatible with one another and difficult to find. I had written the outline of my family history as well as the preface and the first chapter. But at one point I became stuck. For a long time, I tried to write more of my father's story, covering a journey over several generations, but I didn't have enough material to work with.

The family members who knew my father best were now few as he was in his 80s when he passed away. However, his nieces, my first cousins, were alive and well and had their own families. Unfortunately for me however, for nearly two decades before my father had passed away, there was little communication between them. They had argued over land and inheritance and left things unresolved. In order for me to be able to fill in the missing information about my father's life, I would need to garner more information about their own lives and especially their mother's once her brother (my father) had left his homeland. I would have to make contact with them anew.

What exactly would I say? How would I describe what I was doing? How would they react? Would they be excited or suspicious? Would they want to divulge any information or details to me? Would they not want to help me as they still held grudges? The questions were endless and I knew that the only way I could find any answers was to begin relations once again.

And so after such a long period of time, my writing helped rebuild a bridge within the family. While I have yet to interview these relatives individually, we have met on several occasions and I have spoken to them about what I am doing.

In fact, and in a rather unexpected manner, I came to reconsider how I write my family history entirely as a result of this reconnection with my father's side of the family.

My mother would regularly ask me how my writing was going since I had bravely announced I was now 'a writer, though not yet published'. On one occasion when we spoke she asked me, out of the blue, when I would be interviewing her. She had asked me so matter-of-factly and I was embarrassed, because up until that point I had not thought it was something which interested her and so had not yet asked her for a single interview. I had, to my credit, bought two notebooks (one each for my father and mother) filled with some 'starter' questions to help get me writing and thinking about the right sort of questions to ask. However, I had only used my father's up until that point.

I had certainly thought to interview my mother and write down her side of my family's story as well; however, up until that point, I had always intended for that story to be separate. Looking back now, I suppose the reason was that I saw my father's story as one of a journey, physical and mental, over a couple of generations during a watershed period of world history, its transcendence of time and physical space making it 'epic'.

But why couldn't my own mother's story be 'epic' as well? And why couldn't I combine the two as they so neatly complemented each other – not just because my parents eventually married, but precisely because my father's covered one side of the Atlantic after 1945 while my mother remained in Europe.

My mother has now been an amazing source of information as I work to integrate her own recollections and information about what life was like back in Bulgaria after the Second World War. This is crucial for me as there are very few personal accounts written about this time in history from that part of the world. In great contrast to the plethora of information provided by former soldiers or citizens from the west, the experience of the ordinary Eastern European from that time has not been well documented.

This is where my writing group continued to come in very handy. Members of the group would often come across books, old or newly released, which would be useful for others. It was in this way that I heard about *The Broken Road*, a personal account of a journey across Europe in the 1930s which brought to light many aspects of a life now long forgotten, one which my father and later my mother knew. This set the tone for discovering more books. As I began to hone in on exactly what I was looking for, I was able to find bits of information in new places.

I discovered websites, which had just begun to be put together, containing old photos of nineteenth- and twentieth-century life in Bulgaria and Eastern Europe. Incredibly, they were an amalgamation of old photos found in libraries or the country's archives or donated by families who had found them amongst their personal possessions and posted them online in the hopes that someone out there could identify the people and places featured. I realised that there were others who were also trying to piece together the past, whether solely for the desire to preserve such a small country's history or for more personal reasons; or, as in my case, to try and bring together the story of two families who, due to historical circumstances, started life anew on the other side of the world.

I have now amassed more information from my mother, having the good fortune to interview her for hours at a time, writing down her answers as well as recording her voice. I found that recording her in her native language of Bulgarian brought up so many more memories, which she described in such a wonderfully colourful and detailed manner. Irrespective of the fact that she is fluent in English, it was the journey in her mind back through her childhood and beyond which was portrayed much more richly for me as a result of her speaking in her native tongue. Our time together has been very special, and she is now the source of all of my information on her side of the family. Where once she would rely on her older sister for any details she may not remember, she unfortunately has only now herself to rely upon as my aunt passed away in March 2016, the second marker of 'time' in this space of five years.

Kristina Tzaneff *was born and raised in Washington, DC to parents of Bulgarian origin. Kristina graduated from the University of Chicago with a degree in Economics and then moved to Europe with a career in consulting. Based in Sofia, Bulgaria, Kristina helped to head up her firm's business in the Balkans in the mid-1990s, a pivotal time of economic transition in the region. Several years later, she moved to London to work in investment banking where she continued to work with the transition economies of Eastern Europe. Kristina received her MBA cum laude in 2004. She continues to work on private investment projects in the region.*

Kristina's first book, The Rose Horizon, stems from her having lived in both the country of her birth and the country of her heritage during poignant times in each country's history. Through this book, she attempts to put together the lost legacy of her ancestors.

VARIOUS CONTRIBUTORS

Printed in Great Britain
by Amazon